Ants

by Ruth Berman
photographs by William Muñoz

Lerner Publications Company • Minneapolis, Minnesota

To Lisa Bingen for all her encouragement
                                        —R.B.

To Mary Lou and Al
                  —W.M.

Thanks to our series consultant, Sharyn Fenwick, elementary science/math specialist. Mrs. Fenwick was the winner of the National Science Teachers Association 1991 Distinguished Teaching Award. She also was the recipient of the Presidential Award for Excellence in Math and Science Teaching, representing the state of Minnesota at the elementary level in 1992. And special thanks to our young helper, Ben Liestman.

Special thanks to DeWaine Tollefsrud, Naturalist, Minnesota Zoo, for his valuable assistance with this book.

Ruth Berman, series editor
Steve Foley, series designer

Library of Congress Cataloging-in-Publication Data

Berman, Ruth.
  Ants / Ruth Berman ; photographs by William Muñoz.
    p. cm. — (Early bird nature books)
    Includes index.
    ISBN 0-8225-3012-0
    1. Ants — Juvenile literature. [1. Ants.] I. Muñoz, William, ill. II. Title. III. Series.
  QL568.F7B443 1995
  595.79'6 — dc20
                                    95-15123

Manufactured in the United States of America
1 2 3 4 5 6 – SP – 01 00 99 98 97 96

Contents

Be a Word Detective

Can you find these words as you read about the ant's life? Be a detective and try to figure out what they mean. You can turn to the glossary on page 47 for help.

antennas	**honeydew**	**metamorphosis**
colony	**larvas**	**pupas**
crop	**mandibles**	**shed**
exoskeleton	**maxillas**	**thorax**

There is more than one way to form plurals of some words. The words antenna, larva, maxilla, and pupa have two possible plural endings—either an e or an s. In this book, s is used when many antennas, larvas, maxillas, and pupas are being discussed.

Chapter 1

These ants are about ⅓ of an inch long. What do ants have in common with other insects?

Thousands of Ants

Ants look like some of the monsters you see in scary movies. But ants aren't as big as monsters. Ants are insects, and they are small.

All insects have some features in common. There are three parts to every insect's body. Every insect has six legs too. And instead of skin, a skeleton covers an insect's body. This outside skeleton is called an exoskeleton (ek-soh-SKEL-eh-ten).

Like other insects, ants have six legs.

There are about 20,000 species, or kinds, of ants. They live almost everywhere in the world. This is the story of the Formica (for-MY-kah) ant.

Formica ants live in large groups. They live everywhere except in polar places, where it's freezing cold most of the time.

This anthill is in the trunk of a dead tree.

Formica ants are just one type of ant. But there are many kinds of Formica ants. This story is about the Formica ants who live in

10

forests. Their homes are called anthills. All the ants in one anthill make up a colony. A colony could have a dozen ants or millions of ants living in it. So some anthills are very big. Insects that live in colonies are called social insects.

Ants are social insects, living in groups called colonies.

At least one queen and many workers live
in a colony. Queens and workers are all female.

*Most of these ants are workers. The ants with wings
are young queens.*

Workers do everything for the colony except lay eggs.

They each have a special job to do. The queen
has only one job. She lays eggs. The workers
do everything else.

Workers carry a grasshopper meal down into their anthill...

...while other workers watch from above.

Some workers go out to find food. They feed the rest of the colony. Some workers are nurses. They take care of the eggs and the baby ants. Some workers take care of the queens.

Some workers build and fix anthills. And some workers fight enemies. Each worker keeps the same job for as long as she lives.

Workers move sticks and dirt around to fix their anthill.

Male ants are alive only in spring. The males and queens are the only ants that can fly. One time each spring, young males and young queens fly together. They fly only once

Males and young queens have wings.

Queens are bigger than the other ants in the colony. Here, males and queens get ready for their one and only flight.

in their lives. After their flight, the males die. And the queens lose their wings. Some queens go back to their colony. And some queens start a new colony of their own. Either way, the queens go deep into the center of an anthill. Now they are ready to lay eggs.

Chapter 2

When an ant hatches, it looks like a white worm. Do you know what this "white worm" is called?

Changes

Ants go through four stages of growth. The first stage is the egg.

Deep inside the anthill, queens lay tiny eggs. They lay a few eggs every day. The baby ants are in their eggs for about 14 days. Then they hatch. Now they are called larvas (LAR-vuhs). This is the second stage.

Larvas do not look like ants at all. They look like white worms. They do not have legs, and they do not have eyes. Nurses take care of them. The larvas live deep inside the anthill with the eggs and queens.

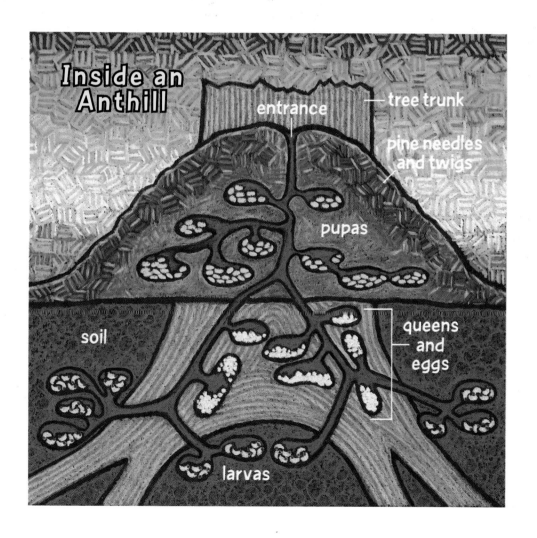

Inside an Anthill

entrance

tree trunk

pine needles and twigs

pupas

soil

queens and eggs

larvas

Larvas grow quickly. Soon they are too big for their skin. The skin splits, and the larvas crawl out. They have just shed their skin.

Larvas are blind and have no legs.

A larva (left) becomes a pupa (right).

Larvas shed four or five times. They keep growing and shedding for up to 20 days. Then they enter the third stage. The larvas spin cocoons and become pupas (PYU-puhs). Pupas live near the top of an anthill.

Finally, after two or three weeks of living in cocoons, the pupas are ready to come out. Now they are adults. This is the fourth stage. The change from egg to adult is called metamorphosis (meh-tah-MOR-fuh-sihs).

Sometimes pupas do not spin cocoons. Then they lie all curled up for two or three weeks, just as they would in their cocoons.

Workers move pupas around to keep them safe and at
the right temperature.

Chapter 3

*All the different kinds
of ants have the
same kind of body.
Can you name the
three main parts of
an ant's body?*

Body Parts

An ant's body is made up of three main parts. They are the head, the chest, and the abdomen.

Two antennas (an-TEH-nuhs) grow out of an ant's head. Antennas are used to touch, taste, smell, and feel movements.

An ant also has two eyes on its head. Ants can't see the same way we do, though. Imagine a mirror smashed into pieces. Images in the smashed mirror would be broken up into bits and pieces. That's how we think ants see the world.

Although ants can see, they use their antennas more than their eyes.

An ant has two kinds of mouthparts on its head too. The mandibles (MAN-deh-behls) work kind of like hands. Ants use their

Mandibles are like jaws, but they move only from side to side. Here, two ants use their mandibles to carry a pupa.

Ants use their maxillas to chew food. Then they squeeze liquid out of the tiny bits of food and spit out the hard parts.

mandibles to dig, fight, and carry objects. But ants don't eat with their mandibles. Ants chew their food with their maxillas (mac-SIH-luhs). The maxillas are behind the mandibles.

Ants can walk upside down because of the two hooked claws on their feet.

An ant's chest is called a thorax. Three legs are attached to each side of an ant's thorax. So, like all other insects, ants have six legs. Each foot has two hooked claws. Ants use their claws to walk up tree trunks. They can even walk upside down.

The abdomen is where food is stored.
There are two stomachs in an ant's abdomen.
An ant has its own stomach and a social
stomach.

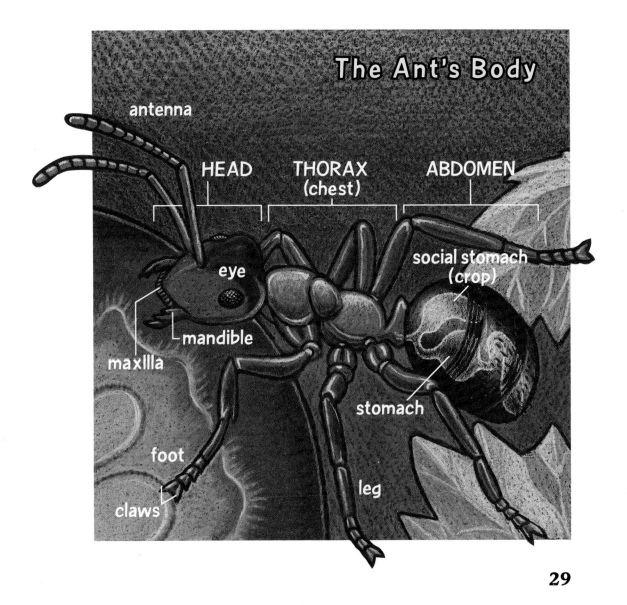

The Ant's Body

antenna

HEAD   THORAX   ABDOMEN
        (chest)

eye

social stomach
(crop)

mandible

maxilla

stomach

foot

leg

claws

Special workers go out to look for food. Some of the food is stored in a worker's own stomach. That food is eaten by the worker herself. But the worker also brings food back

Ants use their antennas to ask other ants for food.

An ant with a full crop feeds a hungry ant.

to the anthill. This food is stored in a pouch called the crop. The crop is also called the social stomach. The worker uses food from her social stomach to feed other ants in her colony. The worker spits up food into the mouths of hungry ants. One ant can feed up to 80 ants this way.

Sometimes ants work together to bring food back to their anthill.

Some kinds of Formica ants can shoot poison from their abdomen. They use poison to kill big insects that they want to eat. They use poison to protect their anthill too. Their poison can be strong enough to make a person faint!

These ants are shooting poison to protect their anthill.
The poison looks like tiny lines in the air.

Chapter 4

These leaf-cutter ants are farmers. What other kinds of ants are there besides farmers?

Ant Life

Different species of ants live their lives in different ways. Some ant species steal eggs from other ants. The kidnappers raise the other ants to be their slaves. Some ant species are farmers. They grow food in their anthills. Some ant species hunt other insects.

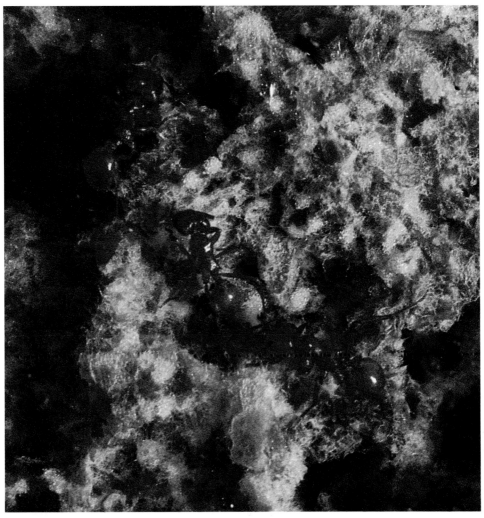

Leaf-cutter ants use leaves to help them grow fungus gardens. These ants are caring for their garden in their underground anthill.

Some kinds of Formica ants collect juice
from insects called aphids (AY-fihds). These ants
use their antennas to tap and stroke aphids.

*An ant strokes an
aphid with her
antennas.*

After stroking the aphid, the ant drinks a sweet drop of honeydew.

The tapping and stroking make liquid sugar drip out of the aphids' bodies. This liquid sugar is called honeydew. Drinking honeydew is a special treat for Formica ants.

Ants are able to pick up objects many times bigger and heavier than they are.

Ants are strong. Formica ants can pick up objects 20 times heavier than they are. Let's say you weighed 50 pounds. And let's say you were as strong as a Formica ant. You would be able to lift a small car!

Ants don't need to be strong to climb straight up, though. The claws on their feet make climbing easy.

Sometimes an object is too heavy for one ant to carry. Then many ants work together. They team up to carry their treasure to the anthill.

It took many ants to kill this grasshopper.

Ants are working together to carry their grasshopper meal to the anthill.

Each of these ants has her own special job, which keeps the whole colony alive.

All the ants in a colony work together. Every ant helps keep the colony alive. Some of these social insects live in your backyard. Next time you go outside, find an anthill. Stay very still and watch the ants. Watch them follow paths. Watch them carry large insects, twigs, and crumbs. Do any of the ants have wings? Now you're a scientist. Now you can enjoy the amazing world of ants.

You can learn more about ants just by watching them in your backyard or in a nearby park.

On Sharing a Book

As you know, adults greatly influence a child's attitude toward reading. When a child sees you read, or when you share a book with a child, you're sending a message that reading is important. Show your child that reading a book together is important to you. Find a comfortable, quiet place. Turn off the television and limit other distractions like telephone calls.

Be prepared to start slowly. Take turns reading parts of this book. Stop and talk about what you're reading. Talk about the photographs. You may find that much of the shared time is spent discussing just a few pages. This discussion time is valuable for both of you, so don't move through the book too quickly. If your child begins to lose interest, stop reading. Continue sharing the book at another time. When you do pick up the book again, be sure to revisit the parts you have already read. Most importantly, enjoy the book!

Be a Vocabulary Detective

You will find a word list on page 5. Words selected for this list are important to the understanding of the topic of this book. Encourage your child to be a word detective and search for the words as you read the book together. Talk about what the words mean and how they are used in the sentence. Do any of these words have more than one meaning? You will find these words defined in a glossary on page 47.

What about Questions?

Use questions to make sure your child understands the information in this book. Here are some suggestions:

> What did this paragraph tell us? What does this picture show? What do you think we'll learn about next? What do all insects have in common? Why are ants called social insects? What are the similarities between your body and an ant's body? What are the differences? Can you name other insects who go through metamorphosis? How many stages does an ant go through to become an adult? What is your favorite part of the book? Why?

If your child has questions, don't hesitate to respond with questions of your own like: What do *you* think? Why? What is it that you don't know? If your child can't remember certain facts, turn to the index.

Introducing the Index

The index is an important learning tool. It helps readers get information quickly without searching throughout the whole book. Turn to the index on page 48. Choose an entry, such as *wings,* and ask your child to use the index to find out what kind of ants have wings. Repeat this exercise with as many entries as you like. Ask your child to point out the differences between an index and a glossary. (The glossary tells readers what words mean, while the index helps readers find information quickly.)

All the World in Metric

Although our monetary system is in metric units (based on multiples of 10), the United States is one of the few countries in the world that does not use the metric system of measurement. Here are some conversion activities you and your child can do using a calculator:

WHEN YOU KNOW:	MULTIPLY BY:	TO FIND:
miles	1.609	kilometers
feet	0.3048	meters
inches	2.54	centimeters
gallons	3.787	liters
tons	0.907	metric tons
pounds	0.454	kilograms

Family Activities

Gently catch some ants and place them in a jar. Put the jar in the refrigerator for about 20 minutes. The cold temperature will slow the ants down. Take the ants out of the refrigerator and observe them through a magnifying glass. What do you see? Make a list of your observations.

While the ants are still in the jar, add some bread crumbs. What do the ants do? Drip a couple of drops of water into the jar. How do the ants react?

Pretend you're an ant. What kind of ant would you be? What would you eat? How would you get your food? Draw a picture of your colony. Include all the workers doing their special jobs. If you were a worker, what would your special job be?

Glossary

antennas (an-TEH-nuhs)—the feelers on an ant's head used to sense touch, taste, smell, and movements

colony—a group of ants that live together and share duties

crop—a pouch used to store food

exoskeleton (ek-soh-SKEL-eh-ten)—the ant's hard, protective covering

honeydew—sweet liquid eaten by ants. Ants get honeydew from aphids.

larvas (LAR-vuhs)—ants in the second stage of their growth. Larvas look like white worms.

mandibles (MAN-deh-behls)—a pair of jaws that moves from side to side

maxillas (mac-SIH-luhs)—small mouthparts used for chewing

metamorphosis (meh-tah-MOR-fuh-sihs)—the changes that ants go through, from eggs to larvas to pupas to adults

pupas (PYU-puhs)—ants in the third stage of their growth

shed—to get rid of old skin. Larvas shed their skin as they grow.

thorax—an ant's chest

Index

Pages listed in **bold** type refer to photographs.